AF505971

UNDER A BALEFUL STAR

ALSO BY VINCE CLEMENTE

Poetry

Snow Owl Above Stony Brook Harbor (1977)

Songs from Puccini (1978)

Broadbill off Conscience Bay (1982)

Girl in the Yellow Caboose (1991)

This Shining Place (1992)

A Place for Lost Children (1997)

Watergaw Along the Thames (1998)

Sweeter Than Vivaldi (2002)

Companions: From a Season of Marriage
(forthcoming)

Criticism

From This Book of Praise (1978)

John Ciardi: Measure of the Man (1987)

Remembering John Hall Wheelock (1991)

Anthology

*Paumanok Rising:
Figures in a Long Island Landscape* (1981)

Selected Prose

Whistling Vivaldi, Singing Whitman: Selected Prose
(forthcoming)

Vince Clemente

UNDER A BALEFUL STAR
A Garland for Margaret Fuller

Drawings by Bill Negron

Cross-Cultural Communications
Merrick, New York
2006

Some of these poems first appeared in the following publications: *Cedarmere Review, Choice, Confrontation, Images, PLA Report of Long Island University, West Hills Review: A Walt Whitman Journal.* "At Mackinaw Island" first appeared in the volume, *Girl in the Yellow Caboose: Remembering Writers.*

Heartfelt thanks to Margaret Pocock, whose sensitive collaboration with Bill Negron served to shape this volume.

Cloth Edition/ISBN 0-89304-147-5
Paper Edition/ISBN 0-89304-148-3

Editor-Publisher: **Stanley H. Barkan**

Cross-Cultural Communications
239 Wynsum Avenue, Merrick, NY 11566-4725/USA
Tel: (516) 868-5635 / Fax: (516) 379-1901
E-mail: cccpoetry@aol.com
www.cross-culturalcommunications.com

First Edition

Cover & Last Page: *Margaret Fuller,* from the 1843 painting by Chappel.

Designed by Tchouki

Printed in Bulgaria by **ANGO BOY**

For my brother and boyhood ally, Albert Clemens

—-Vince Clemente

I would that I could . . . give the lights and the shades,
the hopes and outlooks that come to me in these strange,
cold-warm, attractive-repelling conversations with Margaret,
whom I always admire, most revere
when I nearest see, and sometimes love—
yet whom I freeze, and who freezes me to silence,
when we seem to promise to come nearest.

—Emerson, *Journals,* October 12, 1841

I pass my days in writing, walking,
occasional visits to the galleries.
I read little, except the newspapers;
these take up an hour or two of the day.
I own my thoughts, quite fixed
on the daily bulletin of men and things.
I expect to write this history,
because it is so much in my heart.

—Margaret Fuller, *Letters from Rome,* 1849

CONTENTS

LIVING WITH MARGARET FULLER (1810-1850)

Around 1970, a young man, living in Rome with my wife and school-age daughters, who attended local Italian elementary schools, mornings on the way to work, I'd walk through Piazza Barberini, where in 1828, a twenty-one-year-old American university student named Henry Wadsworth Longfellow read Dante in Italian for the first time. I'd walk through the Piazza, where Hawthorne completed his novel, *The Marble Faun;* and where the year, 1849-1850, Margaret Fuller, also a New Englander and close friend of Emerson, lived with her Italian husband, Count Ossoli, and infant son, Nino, before leaving for their journey back to the United States, that ended, tragically, shipwrecked, off the coast of Fire Island. The family was lost, with only the child's body washed to shore, to be buried by local Fire Islanders on an inland dune.

The plaque, commemorating the grief-ridden tragedy, I fear, is no longer there. However, winters, when the shoreline is desolate, I've traveled from my Sag Harbor home to the scene of the July 1850 catastrophe; and I'm convinced Margaret, Ossoli, and the child remain there as resident spirits. (Week of the sinking of the *Elizabeth,* a frantic and bereaved Emerson sent Thoreau to comb the Fire Island shoreline, and, "To return with something of Margaret's—anything!" A dutiful Thoreau returned with nothing. In fact, Margaret's manuscript of her just-completed *History of the Italian Revolution,* possibly her finest work, was never found.)

In a sense, this volume is an ongoing "conversation" with one, onced described by Van Wyck Brooks as, "Not so much a great woman-writer, as a great woman writing"; one, nonetheless, a critic, literary historian, diarist, translator, editor of Emerson's literary journal, *The Dial,* and foreign correspondent for Horace Greeley's *New York Tribune,* chronicling the events in Italy that had constituted its war for independence. She is also remembered as the early Feminist writer, whose *Woman in the Nineteenth Century* is as poignant today as it was the year it was published in 1845.

This slim volume is also a garland, poems for the nurse-director of the Rome Hospital of the Fate Bene Fratelli during Italy's War of Unification, the American woman, who spoke perfect Italian, and one remembered by the wounded Italian soldiers as "a mild saint and a ministering angel." (Eldest of nine children, she served as the Massachusetts family's "ministering angel," especially after her father's early death. She shouldered every burden, all the while nurturing one of the most far-reaching intellectual minds of the nineteenth century: her own.)

I must add, the art work of Bill Negron inspired me to take a fresh look at the poems and to rework many of them as his artist's vision nudged me to aspects of Margaret Fuller's life and complex self I never quite engaged.

In a real sense, then, this volume is a collaboration, a joint act of homage.

—Vince Clemente

July, 2005
Sag Harbor, New York

I. *Margaret Fuller to Her Mother*

Mother, can you see
the bud about to open,

periwinkle blossom
of a delicate hue,

and the brash geranium, stipple-pink
like the blush on a young girl's face,

or the laurustine, butter-colored,
that spiral their way to heaven?

Why, I hear such flowers blossom in winter,
Mother; I've been told such a thing.

Mine in the garden, the footpath
below the shed, I fear are barren,

with not a leaf on them, nor a single blossom
to hold against my breast,

place under my pillow, summon the angels
there, chittering beyond the meadowfence.

II. *Rye Bread Days*

> *Margaret,*
> *be certain*
> *the children*
> *have learned their lessons*

> *and write*
> *as only you can*
> *sweetly, sweetly*
> *to Father,*

> *and help*
> *with the mending,*
> *your party dress*
> *tattered and shorn.*

> *And those heliotropes*
> *lolling in the garden*
> *forlorn, speak to them*
> *as only you can.*

> *I sense an early frost*
> *do you? Some cord wood*
> *for the shed,*
> *soon, now soon.*

And remember,
apple tarts
for Ellen, her birthday,
tomorrow, noon.

Diary, dear Diary,
these are rye bread days;
all awash in family chores
I'm already behind.

No time
for birdsong
for the nuthatch
nesting under the eaves.

And at night
with only the whip-poor-will awake
and stars so low
my heart heaves, starbruised,

I'll cry myself to sleep
softely, softly
so no one
need listen.

III. *At the Greek School*

Now, what that child wouldn't do!
Bad enough she's a head taller
than anyone at school—

but in a hood! Why not a basket
filled with hickory nuts
lashed to her back?

Why, who ever heard—
porting books
in her cloak's hood,

and the cloak, a cavernous bunt,
a skiff rocking
in the tideswell.

I love best the walk home
at dusk, just before
the first frost,

with forest duff
heaving under me,
the woods, a drizzly hue,

the books, like children
frolicking
along my shoulders,

now raised so high
they place
the fallen vireo's egg

snugly,
back into
its trembling nest.

IV. *Prairie Stillness*

Wickapee, the child said,
  and again, *Wickapee,* pointing
to a prairie flower so lustrous
  I had to shield my eyes.

Now, at night, alone
  on the roof of a prairie cottage,
with thatch as soft as down,
  and sweet as timothy,

I see there are no tree-
  shadows, no mountains
like sleeping lavender birds,
  only starlight along the lake:

just water
  and earth,
but enough space
  for the heart to rest.

V. *At Mackinaw Island*

Dawn, a russet wingbar
  above the lake, the Chippewa
  leave their tents, gods
dance under their eyelids.

A boy up all night
  plays a courting melody
  on a Winnebago pipe
as a girl

dyes linen
  indigo
  in a birch bunt
for her wedding shawl.

Margaret brushes her hair
  runs her hand along the hollow
  below her ribcage. She is 33
and cannot sleep nights;

her womb
  as empty
  as a church
after matins.

VI. *River Walk with Emerson*

He hadn't heard a word.
I couldn't have been talking
to the embers dying in the hearth
as he gazed beyond the window,
beyond the orchard itself
so it seemed.

Imagine,
try to imagine, Margaret,
the moonlight on the river,
he whispered like a man
waking from a dream, sleep
pleaching his eyelids.

A sure-footed Chippewa
and steady as a rhumb line,
he found the path
near the swamp cedar
that sloped down to the river.
I followed, prayerful, in the descent.

Now, Margaret,
see how the moon
clefts the water,
like silver pickerel,
or spiral nebulae, drifting
far beyond the earth's rim.

He pressed my hand
neigher father nor friend,
yet something more.
For as he spoke,
I felt his body shake—
so help me.

And just who was this,
carrying on, as if he were
a young man reeling
from his first kiss:
so young, so frail—
such innocence.

VII. *The Wedding Night*

Even now, you remember
having written,
I have no child
and the woman in me

so craves this, it seems
the want of it
must paralyze me
evermore.

But this night, Margaret,
the hymen broken
what the Greeks called
kleitoris, "a small hill,"

he found you
and worlds from Cambridge:
a rising cairn
in the wilderness.

VIII. *From Rieti: Letter to Waldo*

Can you hear the bells
of the Church del Purgatorio
strike noon, gaffing
the mountain solitude
where snow lingers
after days of hottest sun,
so hot, peasants in the field
run for shade, cry out,
Non posso più resistere.

Waldo, I will not resist this life;
these people I could live with.
Bread and grapes would suffice
and at dusk, to walk
through almond groves,
then watch the sun tumble down
the foothills, nights so cold
you shiver under a shawl,
then a long, blue sleep

in sheets
 washed
  in lime-
   water

IX. *With Nino, Awake*

Child, like me, awake.
Is it the fragrance of camellia
lolling in the onyx vase,

the riverswirl
under
the *loggia?*

Can you see
the last light
on the barricade wall

where your father sleeps,
prays death stay him
another day?

I'll open the shutters, sweet thing,
now, breathe in—hurry,
breathe in the mountain air.

Please, my Nino,
stay with me, in my arms
till morning.

The sun will come,
you'll see,
a toy soldier

carrying in his rucksack
silver stars
that runnel down

the tawny mountains,
high above
Rieti.

X. *From a Bedroom Window in Rieti*

My *Caro Giovane,*
is that you
all night
through the mountains,
stone by stone
a man scaling a dream,
home to me?

Is that you
in the almond grove
kneeling in deep
shadows, blood
from a musket wound,
a sash along your ribcage,
home to me?

No! It's only a lamb,
you know the one I mean,
who strayed from the flock,
more frightened, it seems
than lost, who thinks
the grove's floor, a river-
bed to drink in,

and so like us,
  stragglers: poor,
    poor thing.

XI. *Song for Nino*

Birbone, can you hear
swallows scrape the rooftop
the river swirl under the *loggia,*
the willow bend:
  arched like you,
  blossom of my longing?

Can you hear the bell
of the Capuchins, the brothers
home for compline. Listen:
it is your song, braiding
  the saffron-colored valley,
  where the shy ewe sleeps

her lamb just dropped,
a knotty blue gentian
glistens, how it shines
and glistens, safe,
  safe for now,
  in the waters of the womb.

XII. *A Dream with Water, Lantern-High*

I've no patience with dreams,
to be cast aside, much the way
one shucks a chestnut,
but this one troubles me—abides.

It came as rain
on the terracotta roof,
fistblows of a man
railing against God,

and then—how does one explain?—
trapped in a diligence to Rome
along the spongy plain, dark,
save for flickering marshlight,

and water lantern-high,
with doors locked against the rising tide.
Sweet Christ! We'll be buried alive,
I heard a woman cry.

Then bodies floated like lily pads.
A child passed under me.
I could not reach for his hand;
I tried with all that was in me.

So close, I saw his lips, blanched
like moles on a laurustine,
and thought of my own child, safe
asleep, above the hills in Rieti.

Pray to the Mother of Christ!
the driver cried.
Then all was still,
the diligence as somber as a hearse.

Bodies floated like mossbunker
raked from the pond's bottom,
or curlews circling, holding
an updraft flight.

Then I woke to my child's cry.
How could he know
I had no milk in my breast
to feed him.

XIII. *The Diligence to Rome*

As slow as geologic time,
so it seemed,
the diligence lumbered down
the steep mountain pass

where spring snow
lay flecked
along the boulders,
the driver coaxing the team,

exhorting them to hold:
to swerve
a foot or less
would mean certain death.

At dusk, it trudged into the valley:
the Italian plains shimmering
like molten silver: ahead,
the roseflow of Michelangelo's dome.

Ecco Roma, the driver cried.
Roma, la bella città they answered.
Margaret felt her heart leap, swore
it was something like love.

XIV. *Ossoli at the Pincian Hill*

From your cleft in the hill
you see through umbrella pines
and billowing rooftops
the city below, pitted
with cannon shells, flares
like yellow jonquils.

You pray the siege be over,
that morning come:
a white camellia
Margaret wears in her hair.
You swear you feel her hand
along your cheekbone,

coarse wool sheets
scraping your body,
her breath, sweet
as convallaria,
morning sun anointing
the bedroom, marital bed.

XV. *Margaret Searches for Ossoli*

The wall, My Lord, the wall,
where they withstood cannonshell.

Now blood trickles down
like freshets into a stream,

and in time it will be
a river of blood.

And who would believe, Eastertide
in the Piazza Venezia

French soldiers genuflect
before the tangled Cross.

Even the most callous
feel the stigmata, tremble

as the broken-
Christ passes. Why is it,

always in Italy,
in the cave of the mouth,

blood settles—
a bitter, bitter gall.

XVI. *Letter to Waldo Under Cannonade*

I read your letter under cannonade
that burst like bellwort,
the kind in the meadow behind the shed.
Did Henry get to pruning this year?

I remember as a child stopping myself
on a stairwell asking, "Margaret,
how came you here;
what shall you do about it?"

Mother said a baleful star
rose on my birth. If that's so,
I'll walk forever
in its onyx glow.

Last night, after hospital watch,
I could not wash blood
from my smock.
The boy from Padua, a shell

through his chest, bled white.
He died sobbing in my arms.
I felt life pass through him
as imperceptible as water

clambering along a stalk.
Waldo, such agony, such pain:
he was young enough
to be my son.

XVII. *Hospital of the Fate Bene Fratelli*

To save them
I would have shorn my hair
cross-stitched veins in my arm,
as here in the wards
I move among them.

If wounds did not heal,
we would all drown
in a river of blood,
I say for no one to hear,
as words clot in my throat.

And, at night, I cannot wash
gangrene from my hair,
and musket-burn
like incense
rises from my pillow.

Hour after hour
certain as first dark,
shells fall in the courtyard.
First, like children wheezing
in their sleep,

then a flint-shower
limbs like pollen
carried off in a gust.
Like birds snared in a bunt,
a boy cries out.

At dusk, in the garden
we swear we smell almond bloom,
watch the sun behind Monte Mario
laving the tents of the French
a russet-hue.

I see a boy crouching,
scrawling a note to someone,
as above him, an eagle soars.
I think of home, the goshawk
circling Greylock in a storm.

XVIII. *How Like Flowers, Their Eyes*

Spring came to Rome this morning
with alpine rose leaning, a rut
in a mountain pass above Abruzzi.
And wasn't that a nuthatch that scraped the sill,
our flat, above Piazza Barberini?

I'll open the window
above the garden,
rot of gangrene and musket-burn
washed in green light, now only
apricot from a distant grove.

And the young men, always them:
how like flowers their eyes.
The one from Rimini, a lithe lupine,
and the one who wept in my arms,
his leg left somewhere

beyond the grassy knoll—
a foxglove, hiding
under a meadowfence;
and there, the boy on a cot
under the mantle—

a joe-pye weed, why, last to bloom
before winter. God only knows:
how like flowers their eyes.
I'll make a bouquet
tied with straw,

place it snugly
under my pillow. I'll sleep,
I'm sure. Heavenly fragrance,
like myrrh—no, the meadow
under Greylock.

XIX. *Garibaldi Leaves Rome*

The wounded like bales of hay
lay wedged in the dung carts,
those who could, the young men,
lumbered behind, all their worldly goods
in kerchiefs, swinging
from leather belts.
The women side-saddled their horses,
prayed for the command to withdraw.

Garibaldi, white tunic, plumed hat,
face of a shepherd down from the mountains—
more faun than man—
stared into a dream that had left him,
a deserter, sick with the first rifleshot.
At his side, Anita, the child in her
shouldering the gloom,
never to see the light of day.

He would bury her
along the Po,
breasts heaving
choking to prayer,
her last words
above the riverswirl:
Per Roma!
Per Italia!

The gates of the city open.
Garibaldi raises his arm.
Avanti! he cries.
Viva la Repubblica! they answer.
They ride off in retreat, just before sunrise
leaving the city to the soldiers of France,
to the Pope in his suite,
at his canonical office, saying matins.

XX. *First Snow: Florence,*
Piazza Santa Maria Novella

A child, to wake
to winter's first snow
with flakes nudging juniper boughs,
berries huddled in nacreous cowls,
trunks all stipple-hued.

But to see it now, first snow
cloak Santa Maria Novella, with blue-mist
rising from the Arno, and Poor Clares
from their hilltop choir-loft, singing
sweeter than reedsong.

This moment,
how fit to die in.
Yes, I wold gladly die
at such a time, if I must.
Santa Maria, pray for us.

XXI. *Leaving Livorno: May 17, 1850*

May sauntered along the Apennines
fragrant with wild strawberry and pasture rose;
the *Elizabeth* anchored in the littoral, steady
and always like the Maine coast.

Margaret, sure-footed along the gangplank
cradled her *Journal* in her billowing sleeve,
ink still wet, strangely doleful
from the morning's entry:

I am fearful
my future on earth
will soon close,
she had written.

She recalled the dream,
water under the diligence
lantern-high, and Ossoli
turning from a kiss, whispering:

It was long prophesied,
from drowning
I would die.
What are we before Fate?

May tumbled down the Apennines
the *Elizabeth* impatient
in the tideswell:
the journey back had begun.

 The* Elizabeth *off Fire Island

The lifeboat from Fire Island Light
  retreated, beaten back by waves
    now dune-high.

The howitzer sling fell short.
  Off by 20 rods, it tumbled
    like a broadbill rent by buckshot.

Then a woman sighed:
  Dear God, please
    don't let us die!

We saw the *Elizabeth* split,
  tunneled by marble cargo
    ploughing its side,

like bone piercing a wound,
  a child torn to pieces
    by a lunatic, escaped from an asylum.

XXIII. *Remnants Along the Tideline*

A desk bleached color of bone,
some stray planks of the *Elizabeth,*
and nudging its way out of sand
like an exotic fish
out of the warm Mediterranean,
Ossoli's travelbag.

How modest its treasure:
a baptismal certificate,
lock of a child's amber hair,
map of the *Campidoglio,*
and a silver brush, solemn
under a patina of onyx.

Shore pirates comb the beach, monkbent
so as not to miss a thing,
while 60 rods offshore, somewhere
the bodies of Margaret and Ossoli
float like starfish or green hands
clasped in prayer.

XXIV. *Burying the Child*

What is this dark line of men?
What is it the youngest
holds in his arms?
Why is he crying?

He holds a child wrapped in sailcoth.
All I can see are his lips,
blue like the heavens, his forehead
a burnished grail.

The Widow Hand stands at the doorjamb,
her sitting room
a dark chapel,
and solemn as a tomb.

The service austere
like the shoreline,
no Catholic *Requiem*,
Amazing Grace must do.

By morning, Hawkins had fashioned
a coffin from a seaman's chest,
clean-gutted
and fragrant as a searose.

And from a bedroom drape
a funeral caul, stitched
by the Widow Hand. Let it be said,
we are a practical clan.

We buried the child on an inland dune,
out of the blows of the sea.
Parts of the *Elizabeth* still
floated shoreward:

a rolling pin, a bolt of cloth,
an oak bed frame,
and a child's toy horse
rocking in the waves.

XXV. *Channing's Report*

Such a fitting close
for a life of storms,
where no safe haven
was ever in reach.

To the very end,
she was ravaged: beach pirates,
the ocean a mad thing
screeched from a frenzied face.

She heard no sea-dirge, no lament,
just the wind in rolling
monotone, an organ note
stuck at the base.

Those final hours
even God turned His face
from her, her solitary walk
along the Via Dolorosa.

SOME WORDS FOR VINCE CLEMENTE

"Your writings and experiences certainly add up to much more than a 'small talent'; you've given your life to many important literary studies and figures—and on the way have proven an extraordinary talent. *Sweeter Than Vivaldi,* for instance, with its wide range of themes and elegant compostiion. The rhythms and meters throughout, whether in occasionally measured lines or free verse are rather rare, in my opinion. I seldom have read lines of free verse, for instance, which break at the right time and contain and hold their words in logical (non-distracting) unity."

—Charles Guenther

"The poems speak so, heart to heart, pulse to pulse, ache to joyful ache of life, its beauty, its grief, its shimmer."

—Kark Shapiro

"And this is why you are one of our important writers: because your speaking voice, natural voice, is your writing voice, too. And this means you have earned by a long life of integrity, such honesty that makes the rest of us listen hard."

—William Heyen

"In *This Shining Place,* like Hardy, Clemente brings off what are ostensibly clumsy coinages which shouldn't work—such as 'heart sextant'—and they become quite perfect in context, enriching a delicately graven and poignant achievement."

—Paul Newman (Cornwall, England)

"The beautiful, revised and expanded, *A Place for Lost Children,* is powerful, potent as truth itself. I use it in my courses at University of Wales, Swansea."

—Peter Thabit Jones (Swansea, Wales)

"[Clemente's] work conveys a reverence for the majesty and mystery of how words conjure buried memories, how they connect the past to the present in sweet and solemn communion. *Sweeter Than Vivaldi* begins with a Preface that beckons the reader to find '. . . song and solace in this volume . . . .' The poems that follow deliver both."

—Mindy Kronenberg

Bill Negron is both a painter and printmaker living in East Hampton, New York. Negron has also traveled widely as an illustrator. His published works include: *The Road to Panama, The Caribbean,* and, with Selden Rodman, *South America of the Poets.*

ABOUT THE AUTHOR

Vince Clemente, a SUNY English Professor Emeritus, is a poet-biographer, whose books include *John Ciardi: Measure of the Man* (University of Arkansas Press), *Paumanok Rising,* and seven volumes of verse, one of which, *A Place for Lost Children,* is a text used at the University of Wales at Swansea. His latest volume, *Sweeter Than Vivaldi,* features the paintings of Ernesto Costa (Cross-Cultural Communications, 2002). His work has also appeared in *The New York Times, Newsday, The Boston Book Review, VIA, The South Carolina Review, Blue Unicorn, Cumberland Poetry Review,* various publications and newspapers in the United Kingdom, as well as in anthologies like *Blood to Remember: American Poets on the Holocaust* (Texas Tech University Press) and *Darwin: A Norton Critical Third Edition.* As a visiting lecturer, he has spoken at Hofstra, C.W. Post, Southampton College, SUNY Albany, Oswego, and Binghamton, as well as at museums like the Heckscher and Parrish and at galleries like the Clayton & Liberatore. For many years he served as a trustee of the Walt Whitman Birthplace and was founding editor of *West Hills Review: a Walt Whitman Journal.* From 1996-1998, he lived in England, where he lectured and wrote. He now lives in Sag Harbor with his wife, Ann, and serves as a columnist for *The Sag Harbor Express. The Vince Clemente Papers* are now part of the Rush Rhees Library, Department of Rare Books & Collections of Rochester University, his Journals & Memorablia, with Smithtown Library's Long Island Room.